Why Coyotes Howl at the Moon

Rob Arego
Illustrated by Vicki Bradley

Rigby
A Harcourt Achieve Imprint

www.Rigby.com
1-800-531-5015

Coyote was very hungry. He had been chasing Rabbit all day, but no matter how fast Coyote ran, he could not catch up to speedy Rabbit. Now it was nighttime, and he needed a new plan to surprise and catch Rabbit. He wanted to take Rabbit by surprise, but he didn't know how.

Coyote sat down on a hill above the pond to think. Suddenly, he got an idea. "If I chase Rabbit to the pond, I can trap him there," he said to himself, "because Rabbit cannot swim." Coyote was pleased with himself. He thought he was very clever.

Coyote's plan worked perfectly. Soon Rabbit was trapped at the edge of the pond.

"I have chased you all day. I finally have you cornered," said Coyote. "You can't escape now."

Rabbit had to think quickly. "Wait! I have a better idea," he said as Coyote was about to catch him. Coyote stopped to listen. He liked good ideas. Rabbit pointed to the pond. "Don't you see that big round piece of cheese in the middle of the pond?" he asked.

Coyote stared into the pond. At first he didn't see anything in it. Then his eyes opened wide as he spotted the cheese. He loved cheese.

"If you swim out to the middle of the pond, you can have the cheese all for yourself," said Rabbit. "That cheese will make a much better meal than a skinny rabbit like me."

Coyote's eyes grew even wider as he thought about eating all of the cheese. Within seconds Coyote dove into the pond and swam as fast as he could toward the cheese. When Coyote reached it, he said, "Now I will take that cheese back to land and eat it all. This will be much tastier than Rabbit."

Every time Coyote tried to bite the cheese with his jaws, water rushed into his mouth. After many tries, Coyote grew tired and swam back to shore. He stood at the edge of the pond and shook the water from his fur. Rabbit quietly laughed at foolish Coyote.

"No matter what I do, I cannot grab the cheese," Coyote cried. "What do you think I should do?"

"I have an idea," said Rabbit. "If you drink all of the water in the pond, the cheese will be waiting for you at the bottom."

Coyote didn't waste any time. He couldn't wait to eat the cheese. He drank and drank and drank. Before long, all of the water in the pond was gone. When Coyote walked out to the middle of the pond, there was nothing there. "What happened to the cheese?" he asked Rabbit.

"Isn't it in the middle of the pond?" Rabbit asked.

"No, it has disappeared," said Coyote.

"Where do you think it went?" asked Rabbit.

"I don't know," said Coyote. "Will you help me find it?"

"No," said Rabbit, "it's getting late, and I want to get home while the full moon is still out."

Coyote looked up high into the sky,
where he noticed the big round moon.
Suddenly, he realized what had happened.

"You tricked me," Coyote cried out to Rabbit. "You told me it was cheese when it was only the moon shining down on the water! Well, I will have the last laugh. Now I will eat you."

"Try to catch me if you can," Rabbit laughed and began to walk away down the trail that was lit by the bright, full moon.

"You won't be laughing when I eat you for supper," said Coyote. But as Coyote started to chase Rabbit, he realized that he could hardly move. Coyote had drunk so much water that his belly was almost touching the ground.

Rabbit laughed and laughed.
"Good night," Rabbit said.
"Maybe I will see you tomorrow."
Coyote sat down by the side of the pond
and began to howl angrily at the full moon.
He howled and howled all night. Coyote
still howls at the full moon every time he
remembers the trick that Rabbit played
on him.